THE KNAVE OF HEARTS

Maxfield Parrish

The Knave of Hearts—a play based on a nursery rhyme made famous through its inclusion in Lewis Carroll's *Alice's Adventures in Wonderland*—was written by Louise Saunders, the talented wife of legendary editor Maxwell Perkins. Saunders's play follows the fanciful story of the royal household of Pompdebile, King of Hearts, as his bride-to-be, Lady Violetta, struggles with a requirement for their marriage. Violetta must bake pastry satisfying to the King. She cannot cook, alas!, but she gets essential help from the royal Knave, and everything works out in the end.

Maxfield Parrish (1870–1966) is remembered today as one of America's greatest illustrators, and his paintings for *The Knave of Hearts*—first published in 1925—are considered masterpieces. Parrish is known for combining luminescent color, photorealism, surreal imagery, and technical excellence.

Twenty-two of Maxfield Parrish's illustrations for *The Knave of Hearts*, including the bookplate and endpaper paintings from the original printing, are included here. The paintings depict the delightful, humorous, and lovable characters in Saunders's play. Most of them relate directly to scenes in the script, but some of them—such as *The Gardener Wheeling Vegetables*, *The Youth and the Frog*, and *Chef between Two Lobsters*—serve as enhancements to the story. All 22 paintings are shown as small pictures on the inside front and back covers. When you color in the line drawings, you might want to copy their colors, or you might decide to use your own. We've left the last page of this book blank so that you can draw and color a picture of your own.

Pomegranate kids®

COLORING BOOK

All works of art are paintings by Maxfield Parrish illustrating Louise Saunders's play *The Knave of Hearts*.

1. *This Is The Book Of* (bookplate from the original edition of *The Knave of Hearts*)
2. *The Characters* (the cast of characters in order of their appearance in the play)
3. *Two Pastry Cooks: Blue Hose and Yellow Hose* (Two pastry chefs belonging to the royal household of Pompdebile the Eighth, King of Hearts, await the arrival of the King in the palace kitchen.)
4. *Entrance of Pompdebile, King of Hearts* (The King impatiently enters the palace kitchen, eager for his intended bride, Lady Violetta, to prove that she can bake pastry—a legal requirement of the Queen-elect.)
5. *Lady Ursula Kneeling before Pompdebile, King of Hearts* (The King questions Lady Ursula as to the whereabouts of her mistress, Lady Violetta.)
6. *The Six Little Ingredients* (After Lady Violetta has been found, six boys enter the kitchen carrying ingredients for the tarts she is about to bake.)
7. *Lady Violetta about to Make the Tarts* (Lady Violetta asks for the tart ingredients in nonsensical order, exposing her ignorance about baking.)
8. *Violetta and Knave Examining the Tarts* (Once the King has left the kitchen, Violetta admits to the Knave that she cannot cook; the two look into the oven hoping for a miracle, and then the Knave runs home to retrieve the excellent raspberry tarts his wife has baked that morning.)
9. *The King and the Chancellor at Kitchen Door* (The King and the Chancellor return to the kitchen at the appointed time and request admittance to test the raspberry tarts.)
10. *The Knave* (Accused of stealing Lady Violetta's pastries, the Knave is discovered sitting under some shrubbery eating a tart made by his wife.)
11. *The King Tastes the Tarts* (After tasting a tart—actually made by the Knave's wife—the King cries to Violetta, "My dear, they are marvels! Marvels!")
12. *The Serenade* (detail) (enhancement to the story)
13. *The Knave Watching Violetta Depart* (enhancement to the story)
14. *Two Chefs at Table* (enhancement to the story)
15. *Two Cooks Peeling Potatoes* and *Chef Carrying Cauldron* (enhancements to the story)
16. *Fool in Green* (detail) (enhancement to the story)
17. *The Gardener Wheeling Vegetables* (detail) (enhancement to the story)
18. *The Youth and the Frog* (detail) (enhancement to the story)
19. *Chef between Two Lobsters* (enhancement to the story)
20. *Romance* (detail) (endpaper for original edition of *The Knave of Hearts*)
21. *Romance* (detail) (endpaper for original edition of *The Knave of Hearts*)
22. *The End: The Manager Bows* (The theater manager takes a final bow.)

Pomegranate Communications, Inc.
Box 808022, Petaluma CA 94975
800 227 1428   www.pomegranate.com

© 2010 Pomegranate Communications, Inc.

Catalog No. CB122

Designed and rendered by Oky Sulistio

Printed in Korea

19 18 17 16 15 14 13 12 11 10   10 9 8 7 6 5 4 3 2 1

Pomegranate Europe Ltd.
Unit 1, Heathcote Business Centre, Hurlbutt Road
Warwick, Warwickshire CV34 6TD, UK
[+44] 0 1926 430111
sales@pomeurope.co.uk

This product is in compliance with the Consumer Product Safety Improvement Act of 2008 (CPSIA). A General Conformity Certificate concerning Pomegranate's compliance with the CPSIA is available on our website at www.pomegranate.com, or by request at 800 227 1428. For additional CPSIA-required tracking details, contact Pomegranate at 800 227 1428.

1. *This Is The Book Of*

THE CHARACTERS

IN THE ORDER OF
THEIR APPEARANCE

THE MANAGER
BLUE HOSE
YELLOW HOSE
FIRST HERALD
SECOND HERALD

POMPDEBILE
THE EIGHTH
KING OF HEARTS
[PRONOUNCED POMPDIBILEY]

THE CHANCELLOR
THE KNAVE
OF HEARTS
URSULA
THE LADY VIOLETTA
SIX LITTLE PAGES

2. *The Characters*

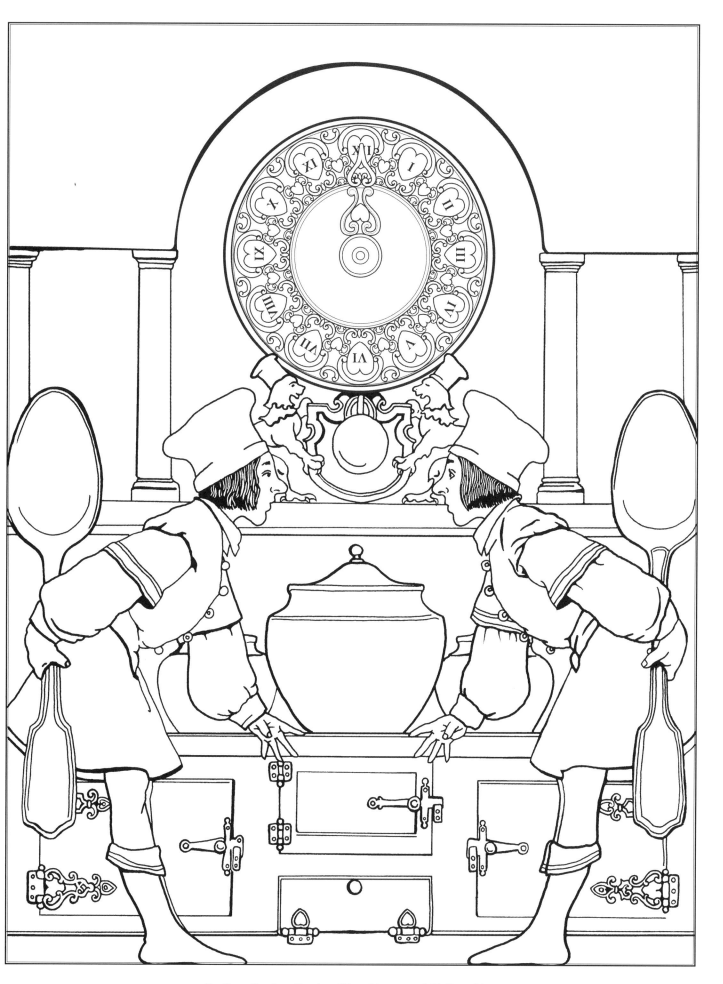

3. Two Pastry Cooks: Blue Hose and Yellow Hose

4. *Entrance of Pompdebile, King of Hearts*

5. Lady Ursula Kneeling before Pompdebile, King of Hearts

6. *The Six Little Ingredients*

7. Lady Violetta about to Make the Tarts

8. *Violetta and Knave Examining the Tarts*

9. *The King and the Chancellor at Kitchen Door*

10. *The Knave*

11. *The King Tastes the Tarts*

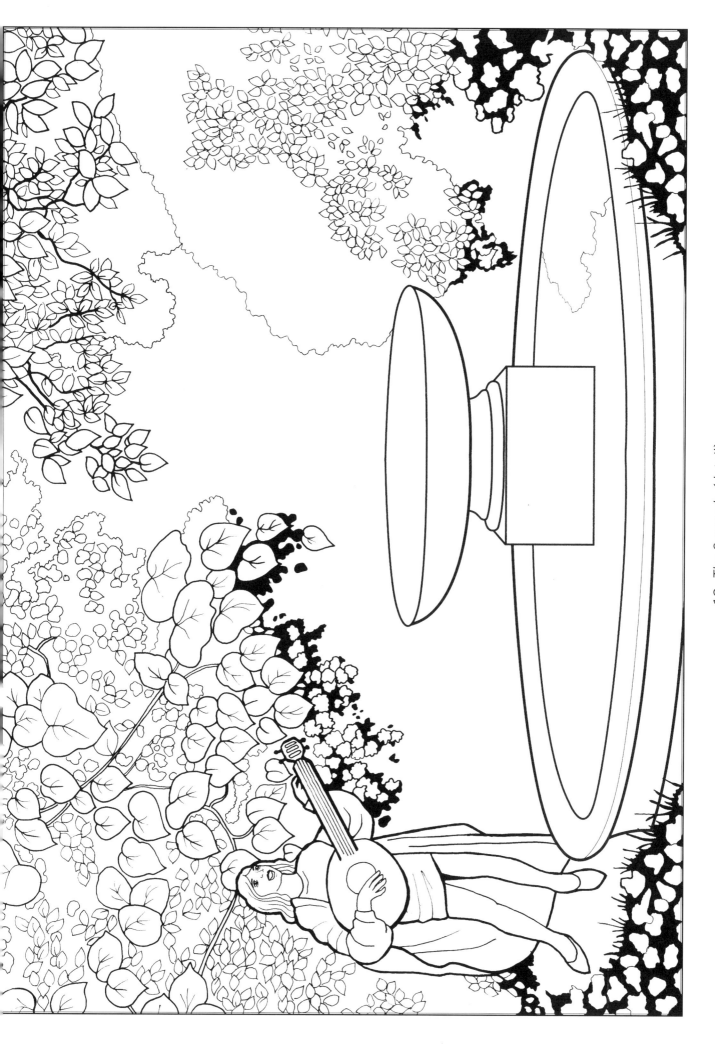

12. *The Serenade* (detail)

13. *The Knave Watching Violetta Depart*

14. Two Chefs at Table

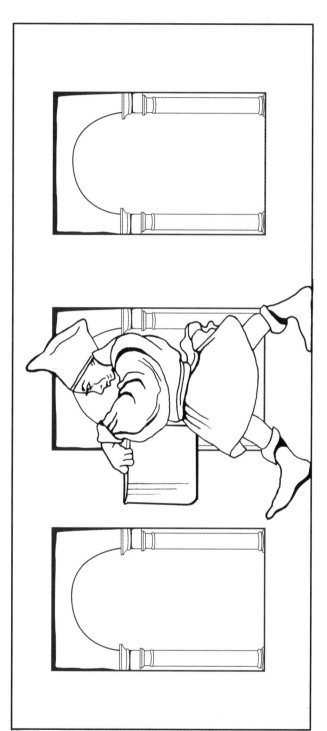

15. Two Cooks Peeling Potatoes and Chef Carrying Cauldron

16. *Fool in Green* (detail)

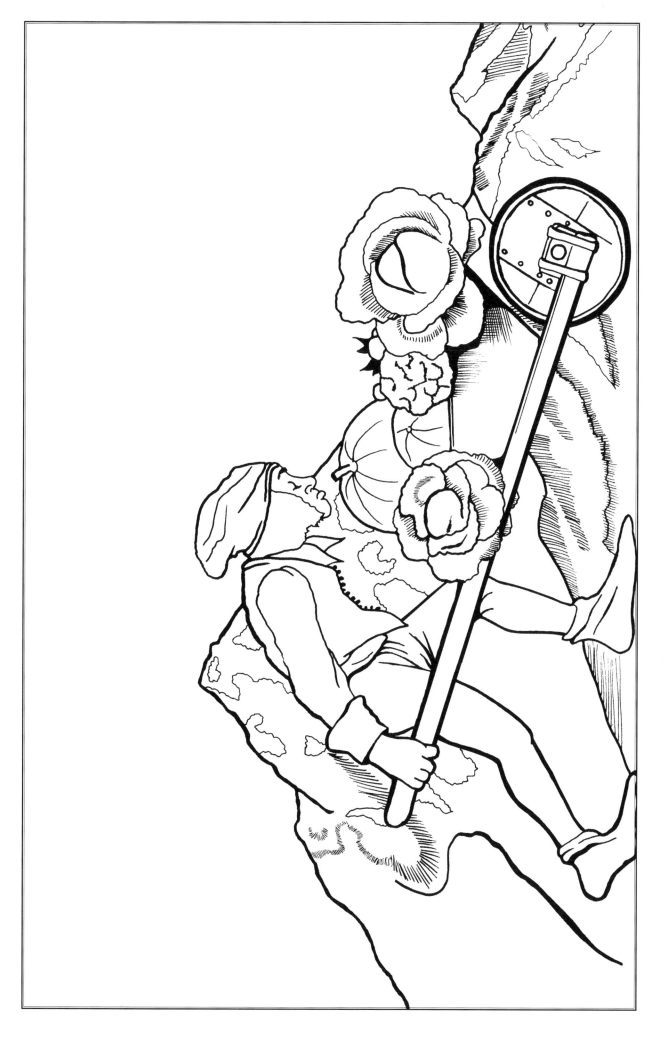

17. The Gardener Wheeling Vegetables (detail)

18. *The Youth and the Frog* (detail)

19. Chef between Two Lobsters

20. *Romance* (detail)

21. *Romance* (detail)

22. The End: The Manager Bows

aw and color your own picture here!